THE
Oh, 'Cause You
OKAZU
Hungry!
GUIDE

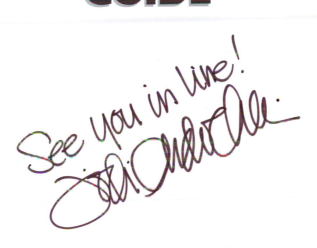

See you in line!

Save a sushi for me!

THE

Oh, 'Cause You

OKAZU

Hungry!

GUIDE

Donovan M. Dela Cruz
Jodi Endo Chai

WATERMARK PUBLISHING

This book is dedicated to the okazuya owners and workers who took the time to talk story with us and participate in this project. Your days are long and the work is hard; your business is truly a labor of love. Thank you for sharing your wisdom and your heart-warming stories — and, most of all, for keeping an important local tradition alive and well.

© 2000 by Donovan M. Dela Cruz and Jodi Endo Chai

Cover by Kelly Sueda, whose oil paintings are available
on Oahu at the Gallery at the Willows and the Diamond
Head Grill and at other locations throughout Hawaii.

Design
Gonzalez Design Company

Production
Wendy Wakabayashi

Library of Congress Card Number: 00-109801
ISBN 0-9705787-0-9

Watermark Publishing
1000 Bishop Street, Suite 501-A
Honolulu, Hawaii 96813
Telephone (808) 587-7766
e-mail: sales@watermarkpublishing.net

Printed in China

FOREWORD
by Chef Sam Choy

In Hawaii, no culture exists in a vacuum. Remember that game we played when we were growing up? All the kids in class would sit in a line, the teacher would whisper something in the first person's ear, and the whisper went from ear to ear down the line, where the kid at the end announced what he or she heard. Of course, it was always something entirely different from the original version!

The premise of Hawaiian regional cuisine is somewhat similar to that old childhood game. The native Hawaiian culture and immigrant cultures converged to produce a unique world unto its own. What naturally followed was our special island cuisine.

Today, in little neighborhoods all over Hawaii, a tradition born of our immigrant cultures is very much alive and well — the okazuya. Before Hawaii became a true melting pot, the different ethnic groups lived apart, but worked and ate together every day. These days, you'll find this collaboration in the okazuyas, where Japanese, Chinese, Korean, Filipino and Hawaiian food — or "just plain local" concoctions like Spam stuffed eggplant or fried chicken skins — are displayed right alongside each other.

Some may see the okazuyas as old-fashioned ingredients in the modern melting pot, but I take my hat off to these folksy little eateries. In *The Okazu Guide: Oh, 'Cause You Hungry*! passionate and persistent okazuya hunters Donovan M. Dela Cruz and Jodi Endo Chai remind us that the chefs of Hawaii Regional Cuisine are part of the legacy of these mom-and-pop establishments. This book isn't just a physical guide to more than 40 okazuyas on the island of Oahu. It is also a nostalgic tour of the traditions that shaped the community we call "local," an important part of the Hawaii we're fortunate to call home.

Let's eat! ('cause I'm hungry!)

ACKNOWLEDGMENTS

Special mahalos to Chef Sam Choy, artist Kelly Sueda, designer Leo Gonzalez, production manger Wendy Wakabayashi and to George Engebretson and Duane Kurisu of Watermark Publishing.

Thank you also to our families: Larry Dela Cruz, Pat Dela Cruz and Donalyn Dela Cruz; and Garrett and Jenna Chai; Harry and Nancy Endo; Serena and David Chai; Cathy, Kurt, Kyra Shaye and Carli Ayn Ing; Kim Chai and David Landry; and Chris Chai.

To Neal Yokota, Sonja Swenson, Annette Chang, Bryan Honda, Dara Fujimoto, Kristy Shibuya and the whole gang at Stryker Weiner & Yokota Public Relations.

To Russell Okata, Randy Perreira, Wayne Yamasaki, Randy Kusaka and the rest of the HGEA family.

And mahalo to Candice Lee, Lance Tomasu, Kacy Nomura, Kenneth and Jan Fukada, Kimberly Hong, Ken Kobayashi, Dana Harvey, Lori Morimoto, Reid Mitsuyoshi, Steph and Jeff Furuta, Jeff Sakai, Lynne Heya, Jon Conching, Kuulei Leslie-Lockwood, Betty Shimabu-kuro, Derek Ferrar, Deborah Gushman, Floyd Ota, Nani Bennett, Franklin Odo, Ernie Tasaki, Janel Nomura, Lee Yoshimura, Craig and Joy Fujikawa, Cindy and Wade Matsumoto, Kathy Hamada-Kwock, Mark Kirimitsu, David Tokuda, Daphne Chung, Rod Tanonaka, Eri Hasegawa, Cy Okinaka, Keith Kamisugi, Laurie Chung, Garret Fujieda, Rob Deveraturda, Noelani Schilling-Wheeler, Mitsue Varley and Lisa Mock.

CONTENTS

v   Foreword by Chef Sam Choy

2   Introduction

6   Glossary

8   Country Okazu

22   Leeward Okazu

36   Kalihi Okazu

56   Downtown Okazu

66   Midtown Okazu

80   Uptown Okazu

90   Windward Okazu

106   Index

INTRODUCTION

Okazu.

The word alone makes your mouth water. All your favorites come to mind — salty ume musubi, tender teri beef, fluffy potato hash patty, tasty chow fun, sweet and spicy kinpira gobo, crispy fried chicken, crunchy-on-the-outside-moist-on-the-inside sweet potato tempura...

If you grew up in the Islands, chances are you've frequented the neighborhood okazuya — maybe before a day at the beach, or before a field trip during small-kid time. You had to get there early for the best selection; there was nothing worse than finding only hot dogs and egg rolls left in the display case. But even if you arrived by 6 a.m., the okazuya was already packed with customers, the line snaking out the door and down the sidewalk. As people went in and out, you'd hear the squeak and slam of the door and think, "Yes! One step closer to getting my okazu!" But if the line was long, the wait wasn't. The okazuya workers were fast and efficient, and no matter how many items you ordered, they could arrange them to fit perfectly in the little rectangular cardboard box.

Okazuya Culture

Before Hawaii Regional Cuisine, before fast food — even before the plate lunch — there was okazu, the unique blend of dishes and delicacies that helps define the Hawaii experience. You find the best okazu at the okazuya, usually a little eatery tucked away in a weathered building or a modest shopping center. Technically, the word is a combination of the Japanese *okazu*, side dish, and *ya*, shop. But in the Islands, the okazuya is much more than just a Japanese food shop. A true product of Hawaii's cultural melting pot, today's typical okazuya is a small family business, out in the country or right in the neighborhood where you live. Humble in origin, sometimes passed along from generation to generation, it is a simple, even nostalgic, Island institution — keeping alive the spirit of a slower, simpler era.

The people who run the okazuyas can be like family — folks who've seen their customers and their customers' kids grow up before their eyes. In fact, eating okazu was an important part of growing up for most locals. It's still a part of our culture, and a big part of our life.

Origins of the Okazuya

How did Hawaii's okazuyas come to be? Since little has been written on the subject, we went out and asked the experts — okazuya owners and okazu lovers. Some believe that early Japanese contract laborers brought the concept with them when they arrived to work on Hawaii's sugar plantations. In Japan, similar eateries called *ekiben* were located at the train stations. In Hawaii, peddlers from the various ethnic plantation camps traveled door-to-door on horse-drawn wagons that carried bento, fresh vegetables and fish.

Others believe the okazuya started when the single plantation laborers paid women in the camps to help with such domestic chores as cooking, cleaning and laundering. The women would prepare bento lunches for the men before they went off to toil in the fields under the hot sun. There the workers shared their lunches, sampling ethnic foods from China, Korea, Portugal, the Philippines and other exotic places around the world.

By 1900 there were more than a hundred Japanese stores throughout the Hawaiian Islands, many of them started with money saved during a worker's contract period. In the 1920s, when contract labor became illegal, more immigrants left the plantations to open shops of their own. Some became tailors and barbers, but others opened grocery stores and okazuyas.

Several sources note that "okazuya" is a plantation word rarely used in Japan today. What Hawaii residents call an okazuya is a *sozaiya* — delicatessen — in Japan.

Even okazuya owners who've lived in Japan say that okazuyas are unique to the Islands. Although some of the okazu items are similar to Japanese food, they point out, the taste can be very different. Hawaii's okazu has a true "local" flavor influenced by many ethnic groups. What's more, Island okazuyas have created and developed their own recipes which have been in each family for generations.

Maybe you've got your own story about the origins of the okazuya. We'd love to hear it if you do; you can reach us by e-mail at okazuyabook@yahoo.com.

Rules of Their Own

Can you imagine a restaurant that closes during family vacations — for up to two weeks at a time? Who would open an eatery with no parking or seating? And what about signage? Shouldn't it be easy to see? Shouldn't there at least be one?

Okazuyas are often the exception to the usual rules of retailing and promotion. The fact is, they made their "rules" before there were any. And we all know them: When visiting your favorite okazuya, you know that the line might be long. Parking might be difficult to find. Driving to an out-of-the-way location is often part of the deal. They might not even replenish your favorite dish when it runs out. But still we go, and keeping going back. And we love it.

Find and Grind!

Sometimes you've just gotta have okazu, whether it's for your child's field trip, a day at the beach, a football game or a potluck with family. But what if your favorite okazuya is closed? Or the food's run out? Or you have to drive around the block for 20 minutes because there's no parking?

What if you're new to the Islands? Maybe you've heard or read about these little hole-in-the-wall food meccas, but you just don't know where to find them.

That's why we wrote this book, for okazuya neophytes and for people like us who won't settle for anything but the real thing. This book will give you the inside scoop on all your favorite okazuyas and introduce you to some you never knew existed. It's a comprehensive guide for the island of Oahu, and it's a workbook too, with room to jot down notes on your favorite items, a secret parking spot, the best time to go or the cost of the prepacked bento. Use it to help hone your skills and become a true okazuya hunter!

So get started — eat your way around the island! Take along some wet-wipes and get messy! Taste everything and, above all, have fun!

Happy hunting!
Donovan M. Dela Cruz
Jodi Endo Chai

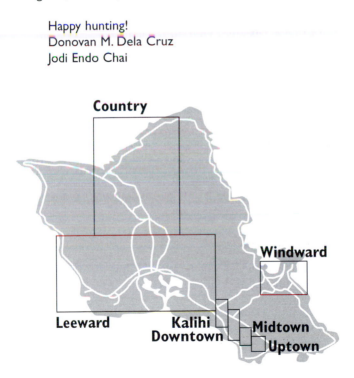

GLOSSARY

adobo	Filipino dish of pork or chicken
andagi	Okinawan doughnut
bento	Japanese box lunch
chow fun	wide noodles stir-fried with vegetables; distinctive local-style dish not to be confused with the traditional Chinese variety
chiso	leaf of the beefsteak plant
guisantes	Filipino dish; meat or poultry cooked with peppers and peas in a tomato sauce base
hekka	meat (chicken, beef or pork), translucent noodles, bamboo shoots and mushrooms simmered in a shoyu-based sauce
inari sushi	more commonly known as cone sushi; sweet vinegar-flavored rice placed inside fried tofu
kabocha	pumpkin simmered in a sauce
kanpyo	dried gourd strips
katsu	breaded pork or chicken cutlet
kim chee	Korean appetizer; hot, salty pickled cabbage
kinpira gobo	burdock (root) sliced thin and sauteed
kobu (konbu)	dried kelp
kobu maki	chicken or pork wrapped in kobu, tied with kanpyo
lechon kawali	Filipino dish; crispy roasted pork
loco moco	rice, hamburger patty and over-easy egg all covered with brown gravy (originated on the Big Island)
lomi salmon	cold salad made with salted salmon, diced tomatoes and diced onions
lumpia	Filipino spring roll; vegetables and ground pork in a thin rice wrapper and deep fried
lup cheong	Chinese sausage

maki sushi	sweet vinegar-flavored rice rolled in nori; sometimes includes items such as egg, kanpyo, carrots and tuna flakes
meat jun	Korean dish; barbecue meat dipped in egg and fried
miso	fermented soybean paste
misoyaki	fish marinated in miso, then grilled
mochi	Japanese rice cake made with sweet rice
mochiko	sweet rice flour
musubi	rice ball
nishime	vegetable stew; includes items such as kobu, carrots, lotus root, bamboo shoots and tofu
nori	roasted seaweed
oyako donburi	chicken and egg on rice
poke	marinated raw fish
pupu	appetizer
saba	mackerel
saimin	thin noodles in broth
tako	octopus
teishoku	set meal; special of the day
tempura	shrimp, sweet potato or vegetables battered and deep-fried
udon	thick wheat noodles
ume	salty picked plum; usually placed in the middle of a musubi
won ton	Chinese dumplings filled with ground pork and sometimes shrimp and vegetables
yakitori	grilled chicken on a bamboo skewer

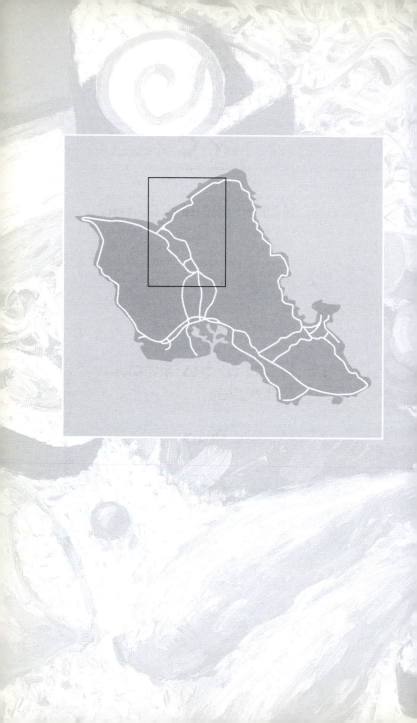

COUNTRY OKAZU

10 North Shore Country Okazu & Bento

12 Sagara Store

14 Kitchen Delight

16 Maru-Hi Restaurant & Lounge

18 Naru's Place

20 Sun's Bar-B-Q

"*My family is originally from the North Shore. We wanted to own our own business and realized Haleiwa didn't have an okazuya. The hours are long and it's hard work, but we're enjoying every minute of it and we love the community.*"

Deann Sakuoka

North Shore Country Okazu & Bento

WHERE STAY?
Haleiwa Shopping Center
66-197C Kamehameha Highway
Haleiwa, Hawaii 96712
Phone 637-0055

HOURS
Monday, closed
Tuesday-Thursday, 6 a.m. - 2 p.m.
Friday, 6 a.m. - 6 p.m.
Saturday, 6 a.m. - 2 p.m.
Sunday, closed

GOTTA GRIND
Fishcake, fried chicken, shoyu chicken

BESIDES OKAZU
Saimin, oxtail soup and pupus. Plate lunch specials offered on Tuesday and Thursday.

SEATING
Make house! (4 tables — but okazu tastes even better at the beach, which is only a few minutes away!)

PARKING
No sweat! (lots of parking at Haleiwa Shopping Center)

CATERING?
Yes

ESTABLISHED
1999

OKAZUYA TRIVIA
North Shore Country Okazu is a family affair owned by two sisters—Janelle and Deann Sakuoka.

NOTES

_____

_____

_____

_____

"The secret to staying in business for so many years is good, loyal customers. The community is one big family. Some people come to visit us straight from the airport."

Colleen Mau

Sagara Store

WHERE STAY?
67-173 Farrington Highway
Waialua, Hawaii 96791
Phone 637-4825
(across Waialua High School —
look for the brown building with
the aluminum roof)

HOURS
Monday-Friday, 5:30 a.m. - 2:30 p.m.
(when school is in session) or
5:30 a.m. - 1 p.m. (during the summer)
Saturday & Sunday, closed

GOTTA GRIND
Inari and maki sushi, fried
chicken, shoyu hot dogs, chow fun,
sweet potato tempura

BESIDES OKAZU
Candies and chips

SEATING
Take-out only!

PARKING
Good luck! (very small parking lot)

INSIDE SCOOPS
Closes for annual vacation sometime
around Christmas.

CATERING?
No

ESTABLISHED
1922

OKAZUYA TRIVIA
Sagara Store is owned by Colleen Mau
and Claire Supebedia.

NOTES
_____
_____
_____
_____
_____
_____
_____

"This is the most enjoyable business for me. I've met so many wonderful people. I wish I had started this business 20 years earlier. I'm getting along in age."

Gladys Okamura

Kitchen Delight

WHERE STAY? 553 California Avenue
Wahiawa, Hawaii 96786
Phone 622-3463
(corner of California and
Walker Avenues)

HOURS Monday-Friday, 5 a.m. - 2 p.m.
Saturday, Sunday & holidays, 6 a.m. - 2 p.m.

GOTTA GRIND Mochiko chicken and teri chicken
(both boneless, skinless), fried saimin,
fish patty, chicken skin chips

BESIDES OKAZU Breakfast, saimin, plate lunch,
Hawaiian food

SEATING Make house! (5 tables)

PARKING No sweat! (street parking along the
building and lots of parking across the
street on Walker Avenue)

CATERING? Yes

ESTABLISHED 1995

OKAZUYA TRIVIA Long-time Wahiawa residents may
remember Kitchen Delight at its former
location on the corner of Cane Street
and California Avenue from 1973 to 1986.
After a fire destroyed most of the
building her okazuya occupied, owner
Gladys Okamura decided to close her
business and focus her energy on
catering. The okazuya itch returned in
1995 when an old neighborhood saimin
shop closed down — it was the perfect
location for her new okazuya.

NOTES _____

_____

_____

"Interestingly, our customers come from all over the island chain. Mostly by word of mouth — a living testimonial to our onolicious food."

Stan Kurio

Maru-Hi Restaurant & Lounge

WHERE STAY?
The Town Center of Mililani
95-1249 Meheula Parkway A-9
Mililani, Hawaii 96789
Phone 623-5848
(in the shopping center with the
movie theaters and Wal-Mart)

HOURS
Monday, 7:30 a.m. - 5 p.m.
Tuesday, closed
Wednesday-Sunday, 7:30 a.m. - 5 p.m.
(The restaurant, which features Japanese
food, is open daily from 11 a.m. - 9 p.m.)

GOTTA GRIND
Fried chicken, fried saimin, chow fun,
inari sushi, kinpira gobo

BESIDES OKAZU
Assorted pre-packed bento. This "okazuya
window" is a part of the Maru-Hi
Japanese Restaurant, which features a
large selection of saimin, teishoku lunch
and dinner specials.

SEATING
Keep your eyes open! (outdoor tables in
the shopping center or in the restaurant
when seats are available)

PARKING
No sweat! (large shopping center
parking lot)

INSIDE SCOOPS
They continue to replenish the food
throughout the day.

CATERING?
Yes

ESTABLISHED
1991

NOTES
_____
_____
_____
_____

"Wahiawa wasn't the first location of Naru's Place. Previous okazuyas were in Pearl City and downtown Los Angeles."

Jay Narusawa

Naru's Place

WHERE STAY?	40 North Kamehameha Highway Wahiawa, Hawaii 96786 Phone 622-4783 (in the unusual-shaped building on an unusual-shaped "peninsula" on Kamehameha Highway next to Zippy's)
HOURS	Monday-Friday, 5 - 11:45 a.m. Saturday & Sunday, closed
GOTTA GRIND	Fried noodles, inari sushi, maki sushi
SEATING	Keep your eyes open! (2 tables)
PARKING	Good luck! (street parking only)
INSIDE SCOOPS	Closes for one to two weeks every year.
CATERING?	No
ESTABLISHED	1987
NOTES	

"When we first opened, there was no okazuya in the area. People came in for breakfast and lunch, and school-children came, too, especially during field trips."

Richard Taltavall

OKAZU *Special*
6 CHOICES $5.65
5 CHOICES 4.80
4 CHOICES 3.95
3 CHOICES 3.25
OVER 5 CHOICES-WHITE RICE FREE

Sun's Bar-B-Q

WHERE STAY?
Mililani Shopping Center
95-221 Kipapa Drive
Mililani, Hawaii 96789
Phone 623-6000
(the shopping center with Blockbuster
Video and Foodland)

HOURS
Daily, 5 a.m. - 2 p.m.
(The okazuya here is part of the
restaurant, which features Korean food
and is open daily from 5 a.m. - 8:30 p.m.)

GOTTA GRIND
Teri beef, fried chicken, chow fun

BESIDES OKAZU
Korean plate lunch (the meat jun is
definitely a "Gotta Grind"), saimin

SEATING
Make house! (7 booths)

PARKING
No sweat! (parking available in the
shopping center)

INSIDE SCOOPS
The food usually runs out by 1:30 p.m.,
so be sure to get there early for the
best selection.

CATERING?
Yes (for small parties)

ESTABLISHED
1980

NOTES

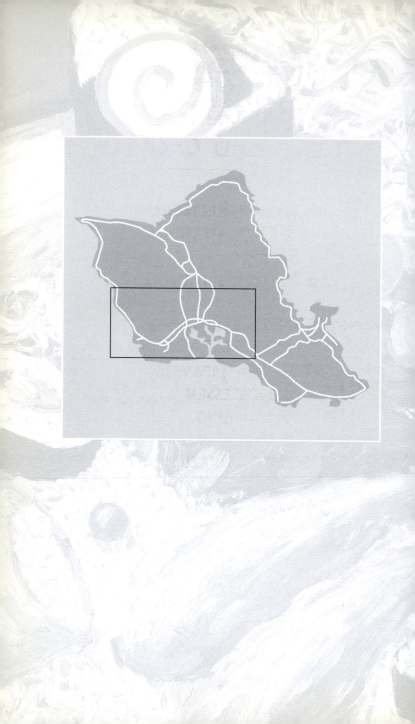

LEEWARD OKAZU

24 KABUKI RESTAURANT & DELICATESSEN

26 MASAGO'S DRIVE INN

28 OMIYA'S RESTAURANT

30 SAKURA JAPANESE DELICATESSEN & CATERING

32 SATO'S OKAZUYA

34 WAIPAHU DELI

"*Our okazuya, I believe, was the first in this area. Without all our loyal employees, we would not have made it 'til today.*"

Katsumi Kazama

Kabuki Restaurant & Delicatessen

WHERE STAY?	Waimalu Shopping Plaza 98-020 Kamehameha Highway Aiea, Hawaii 96701 Phone 487-2424
HOURS	Daily, 5:30 a.m. - 1 p.m. (The okazuya window is part of Kabuki Restaurant: lunch from 11 a.m. - 1:45 p.m.; dinner from 5 - 9:15 p.m. Monday-Friday, 5 - 8:45 p.m. Sunday)
GOTTA GRIND	Inari sushi, maki sushi, kinpira gobo
BESIDES OKAZU	Sushi bar and other Japanese food
SEATING	Take-out only!
PARKING	No sweat! (Waimalu Shopping Center parking lot)
INSIDE SCOOPS	Closes every year Jan. 1 - 2. For those who love nostalgia, Kabuki is one of the few okazuyas that can package your okazu in the traditional paper bento box.
CATERING?	Yes. Private party rooms are also available.
ESTABLISHED	1965
NOTES	

"Although I enjoy owning an okazuya, I also love painting and singing karaoke. I enter karaoke competitions and have even won a few! My artwork is displayed at my drive-in."

Masako Aona

Masago's Drive Inn

WHERE STAY?	85-956 Farrington Highway Waianae, Hawaii 96792 Phone 696-7833 (Can't miss the large pink building on Farrington Highway; look for the rotating sign in the parking lot across from the Waianae Police Station.)
HOURS	Monday-Friday, 4:30 a.m. - 8 p.m. Saturday, 6:30 a.m. - 8 p.m. Sunday, 6 a.m. - 8 p.m. (Even after the okazuya window of Masago's closes, the drive-in stays open — until 11 p.m. Monday through Saturday, until 8 p.m. on Sunday.)
GOTTA GRIND	Long rice, pork with eggplant, teri butterfish, fried noodles, fried chicken
BESIDES OKAZU	Hawaiian food, plate lunch, burgers and breakfast items. Be sure to try the lilikoi juice — refreshing on those hot, sunny Waianae days!
SEATING	Make house! (12 tables — but the okazu will taste even better at one of the nearby beaches)
PARKING	No sweat! (large parking lot)
INSIDE SCOOPS	The food is replenished throughout the day.
CATERING?	Yes
ESTABLISHED	1955
NOTES	_____ _____ _____ _____

"My parents started the business in 1953. My mom and I are still working, and she is 84 years old."

Warren Omiya

Omiya's Restaurant

WHERE STAY?   Aiea Town Square
99-080 Kauhale, Building A-2
Aiea, Hawaii 96701
Phone 486-3773
(in the shopping center next to
Aiea Public Library)

HOURS   Monday-Friday, 6 a.m. - 2 p.m.
Saturday, 8 a.m. - 2 p.m.
Sunday, 8 a.m. - 2 p.m.

GOTTA GRIND   Inari sushi, maki sushi

BESIDES OKAZU   Old-fashioned-style hamburgers,
hamburger steak plate lunch

SEATING   Make house! (6 tables)

PARKING   No sweat! (lots of parking in the
shopping center)

INSIDE SCOOPS   Food usually runs out around 1 p.m., so
get there early for the best selection.
Closes for vacation from Jan. 2-6. Every
Wednesday senior citizens receive a
10% discount.

CATERING?   Yes

ESTABLISHED   1953 (at current location since 1997)

NOTES   _____

_____

_____

_____

_____

_____

_____

"Although I had 15 years of restaurant business experience under my belt, I had never cooked until we opened Sakura. Now I cook almost everything!"

Lloyd Sakuda

Sakura Japanese Delicatessen & Catering

WHERE STAY?	Aiea Town Square 99-080 Kauhale, Suite C1 Aiea, Hawaii 96701 Phone 484-1141 (in the shopping center next to Aiea Public Library)
HOURS	Monday, closed Tuesday-Friday, 5:30 a.m. - 7 p.m. Saturday, 6:30 a.m. - 7 p.m. Sunday, 6:30 a.m. - 1:30 p.m.
GOTTA GRIND	Mochiko chicken, Spam musubi, seafood casserole, chiso musubi, misoyaki butterfish
BESIDES OKAZU	Tofu salad, Oriental chicken salad, assorted bento, plate lunch
SEATING	Make house! (4 tables)
PARKING	No sweat! (lots of parking in the shopping center)
INSIDE SCOOPS	Closes for vacation the first week of January. They accept local personal checks, and they continue to replenish the food throughout the day.
CATERING?	Yes
ESTABLISHED	1993
NOTES	_____ _____ _____ _____

"I closed my okazuya for awhile a few years ago and when I reopened my customers were most appreciative. Mainland visitors also call to order fried noodles, and if they don't have a rental car, they'll catch the bus."

Misao Sato

Sato's Okazuya

WHERE STAY?	235 Hanawai Circle Waipahu, Hawaii 96797 Phone 677-5503 (on the street between Farrington Highway and the old Waipahu Sugar Mill — near the old Big Way supermarket)
HOURS	Monday-Friday, 7:30 a.m. - 2 p.m. Saturday, 7:30 a.m. - 1 p.m. Sunday, closed
GOTTA GRIND	BBQ stick, "old-fashioned" fried noodles, shrimp tempura, sweet potato tempura, inari sushi
BESIDES OKAZU	Won ton min, saimin, plate lunch
SEATING	Make house! (3 tables)
PARKING	No sweat! (lots of parking)
INSIDE SCOOPS	Get there before 11:30 a.m. for the best selection. However, their famous fried noodles are available upon order.
CATERING?	Yes
ESTABLISHED	1965 (at this new location since October 1999)
OKAZUYA TRIVIA	Movie star Matt Dillon once stopped by for won ton min. Elvis Presley was also a patron and sent owner Misao Sato a postcard to thank her.
NOTES	_____ _____ _____ _____

"It's definitely a family business. I first worked with my sister at a concession at Leeward Bowl, then I started Waipahu Deli in 1982."

Cullen Nakama

Waipahu Deli

WHERE STAY?	94-172 Leoleo Street Waipahu, Hawaii 96797 Phone 680-9195 (in the Waipahu industrial area, across the street from City Mill)
HOURS	Monday-Saturday, 5 a.m. - 2 p.m. Sunday, closed
GOTTA GRIND	Mochiko chicken, garlic chicken and teriyaki butterfish
BESIDES OKAZU	Filipino dishes, Hawaiian plate lunch
SEATING	Make house! (lots of tables, and even a television set inviting you to sit, enjoy the food and relax)
PARKING	No sweat! (lots of parking)
CATERING?	Yes
ESTABLISHED	1982
OKAZUYA TRIVIA	All in the family: owner Cullen Nakama's brother Daryll owns the Mitsuba okazuya in Kalihi, while his brother Fred owns Meg's Drive-In, also in Kalihi.
NOTES	

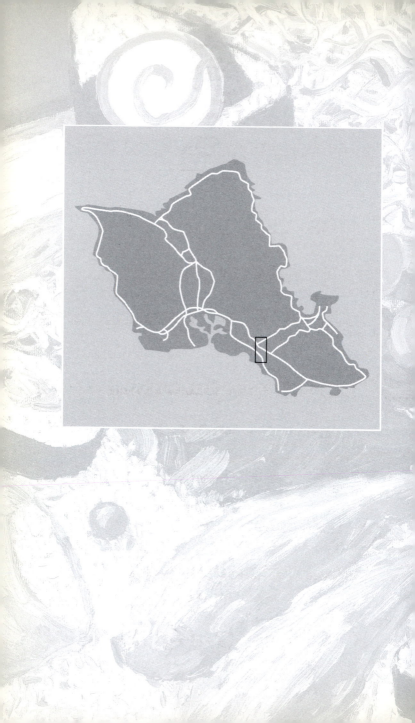

KALIHI OKAZU

38 GULICK DELICATESSEN

40 KAWAKAMI DELICATESSEN

42 MITSU-KEN OKAZU
& CATERING

44 MITSUBA DELICATESSEN

46 NICKY BBQ & OKAZU

48 OKAWA'S OKAZUYA

50 SUGOI

52 TOSHI'S DELICATESSEN
& RESTAURANT

54 YUKI'S COFFEE HOUSE

Gulick Delicatessen

Where Stay?	1512 Gulick Avenue Honolulu, Hawaii 96817 Phone 847-1461 Fax 848-0391 (where you'd least expect it — in the middle of a Kalihi residential area; nearest cross street is North School — just look for the Tasty Chop Suey Chinese restaurant and Fastop convenience store on the corners)
Hours	Monday-Saturday, 4:30 a.m. - 3:30 p.m. Sunday, 8 a.m. - 3:30 p.m.
Gotta Grind	Hash patty (sized for 2 people — it's huge), shoyu butterfish, California roll, and anything fried (tempura, chicken — don't know how they keep it so crispy!)
Besides Okazu	Some Filipino and Chinese dishes
Seating	Take-out only! (suggest you enjoy your food at nearby Moanalua Gardens or Kalihi Park)
Parking	Happy hunting! (street parking only)
Inside Scoops	Especially during lunch hour, it gets crowded so be sure to remember to take a number. It also helps to have your order in mind. They also accept VISA and MasterCard.
Catering?	Yes
Established	1970
Notes	_____ _____ _____

"*Originally, our family had a small mom-and-pop grocery store. During World War II, the soldiers used to stop in to buy sandwich and cold soda. Then my mother decided to make sushi, and she gradually added more okazu dishes.*"

Joyce Arakaki

Kawakami Delicatessen

WHERE STAY?   237 Kalihi Street
Honolulu, Hawaii 96817
Phone 845-8102
(Kalihi industrial area on the corner of
Kahai and Kalihi Streets — look for the
yellow and black sign)

HOURS   Monday-Friday, 5:30 a.m. - 1:30 p.m.
Saturday, 6 a.m. - 1 p.m.
Sunday, closed

GOTTA GRIND   Mac/potato salad, shoyu butterfish,
maki sushi and inari sushi

BESIDES OKAZU   Oxtail soup (Fridays only)

SEATING   Make house! (3 tables)

PARKING   No sweat! (parking on Kahai Street)

INSIDE SCOOPS   Closes from Jan. 1 for about 2 weeks

CATERING?   Yes

ESTABLISHED   1955 (at current location since 1966)

NOTES

"We're still here because of luck and a lot of hard work. I always count my blessings."

Lyle Nonaka

Mitsu-Ken Okazu & Catering

WHERE STAY?
1223 North School Street
Honolulu, Hawaii 96817
Phone 848-5573
Fax 848-5521
(across Liliha Saimin and
Mitsuba okazuya)

HOURS
Monday-Friday, 4:30 a.m. - 1 p.m.
Saturday, 4:30 a.m. - noon
Sunday, closed

GOTTA GRIND
Garlic chicken, shrimp tempura, chicken
yakitori stick, sweet potato tempura

BESIDES OKAZU
Assorted bento, andagi (regular and poi),
plate lunch specials (stuffed cabbage,
turkey, etc.), and their breakfast
special (fried rice and egg — and
inexpensive, too!)

SEATING
Keep your eyes open! (2 outdoor tables)

PARKING
Happy hunting! (2 parking stalls next to
the okazuya and street parking; don't
park on the street 6:30-8:30 a.m. or
you'll get a ticket.)

INSIDE SCOOPS
Although they don't close when the food
runs out, be sure to get there early for
the best selection!

CATERING?
Yes

ESTABLISHED
1993

OKAZUYA TRIVIA
Mitsu-Ken is owned by Lyle Nonaka and
Brad Kaneshiro

NOTES
_____

_____

_____

_____

"I love the freedom to create new items for our customers."

Daryll Nakama

Mitsuba Delicatessen

WHERE STAY?
1218 North School Street
Honolulu, Hawaii 96817
Phone 841-3864
(Just look for the sign standing in the
parking lot — it features a musubi
cartoon character. Mitsuba is across
Mitsu-Ken okazuya.)

HOURS
Monday, closed
Tuesday - Sunday, 5 a.m. - 1 p.m.

GOTTA GRIND
Hot dog musubi, fried chicken, butterfish,
Okinawan sweet potato crumble

BESIDES OKAZU
Breakfast food, plate lunch and the
Nanakuli — a larger version of the
loco moco

SEATING
Take-out only!

PARKING
Good luck! (parking lot fills up fast)

INSIDE SCOOPS
Food usually runs out before closing,
so get there early for the best selection.

CATERING?
Yes

ESTABLISHED
1983

NOTES
_____

_____

_____

_____

_____

_____

_____

"Taking care of my customers is first, even before thinking about money. Service is what keeps us going."

Darrell Siu

Nicky BBQ & Okazu

WHERE STAY?
1150 North Nimitz Highway, Unit C
Honolulu, Hawaii 96817
Phone 533-2563
(behind Nimitz Business Center, the
shopping center with the red awnings)

HOURS
Monday-Friday, 5:30 a.m. - 4 p.m.
Saturday & Sunday, closed

GOTTA GRIND
Mochiko chicken, fried chicken, shoyu
chicken, tempura

BESIDES OKAZU
Burgers, sandwiches, plate lunch
(oyster sauce chicken, steak with
fried rice, garlic chicken, shrimp scampi)

SEATING
Keep your eyes open! (3 small tables)

PARKING
No sweat! (parking on the private road
behind Nimitz Business Center)

CATERING?
Yes

ESTABLISHED
1991

OKAZUYA TRIVIA
They also operate three lunch wagons —
at the airport, on Middle Street and
across the Neal S. Blaisdell Center —
featuring different entrees daily.

NOTES
_____

_____

_____

_____

_____

_____

_____

_____

*"I have good customers.
They have become
like family. I enjoy
cooking for them."*

Betty Okawa

Okawa's Okazuya

WHERE STAY?
414-D Mokauea Street
Honolulu, Hawaii 96819
Phone 847-0944
(one block Diamond Head of Oahu
Community Correctional Center)

HOURS
Daily, 5:30 a.m. - 2 p.m.

GOTTA GRIND
Garlic baked chicken, miso chicken,
teri pork

BESIDES OKAZU
Thai and tofu salad, plate lunch (hekka,
stir fry — menu changes monthly),
Hawaiian food

SEATING
Make house! (4 tables)

PARKING
Happy hunting! (street parking only)

INSIDE SCOOPS
Closes for the week from Christmas
through New Year's Day. Does not
close when food runs out; they continue
to replenish.

CATERING?
Yes

ESTABLISHED
1994

NOTES

"It was our dream from high school to be our own boss. Zach and I had lunch one day and decided to make our dream a reality. We've been saving for this for several years."

Ross Okuhara

Sugoi

Where Stay?	1286 Kalani Street, Building B, Suite 106 Honolulu, Hawaii 96817 Phone 841-7984 (the new shopping complex where GEM used to be; near the Motor Vehicle Division/Satellite City Hall in Kalihi)
Hours	Monday-Friday, 5:30 a.m. - 2:30 p.m. Saturday, 8 a.m. - 4 p.m. Sunday, closed
Gotta Grind	Mochiko chicken, garlic chicken, fried rice, chicken katsu, garlic ahi
Besides Okazu	Tofu salad (a "Gotta Grind"), breakfast from 5 - 10 a.m., assorted bento, salads (somen, pasta, Caesar), plate lunch
Seating	Make house! (2 tables, counter with five bar stools)
Parking	No sweat! (large parking lot)
Inside Scoops	Checks accepted only for large catering orders.
Catering?	Yes
Established	2000
Okazuya Trivia	Sugoi is owned by Zachary Lee and Ross Okuhara.
Notes	

51

"*My Aunt Takako, my mom — Kiyomi — and I do it all: cooking, serving and cleaning.*"

Thomas Kakemoto

Toshi's Delicatessen & Restaurant

WHERE STAY?	1226 North King Street Honolulu, Hawaii 96817 Phone 841-6634 (across the Kapalama post office)
HOURS	Monday, closed Tuesday-Friday, 4:30 a.m. - 12:30 p.m. Saturday & Sunday, closed
GOTTA GRIND	Teri hamburger, fried chicken, mac salad, fish cake, shoyu chicken and tofu with gravy
SEATING	Make house! (6 tables)
PARKING	Happy hunting! (street parking only)
INSIDE SCOOPS	They usually sell out of items fast, so get there early for the best selection.
CATERING?	No
ESTABLISHED	1961
NOTES	

"We put in 12 hours a day. There is no end to this kind of work. When customers tell us the food taste good, we feel happy."

Kenichi Shibuya

YUKI'S
OKAZU - BENTO
TEL 842-6046

Yuki's Coffee House

WHERE STAY?	1320 North School Street Honolulu, Hawaii 96817 Phone 842-6046 (across Kamehameha Bakery; one block from Mitsu-Ken)
HOURS	Monday-Saturday, 7 a.m. - 4:30 p.m. Sunday, closed
GOTTA GRIND	Stuffed mahi and stuffed shrimp, spinach roll, lumpia, hash, kabocha
BESIDES OKAZU	Oyako donburi, plate lunch, burgers, saimin
SEATING	Make house! (6 tables)
PARKING	Happy hunting! (4 parking stalls and street parking)
INSIDE SCOOPS	Closes on Christmas and New Year's Day — but available for catering anytime.
CATERING?	Yes
ESTABLISHED	1988
NOTES	

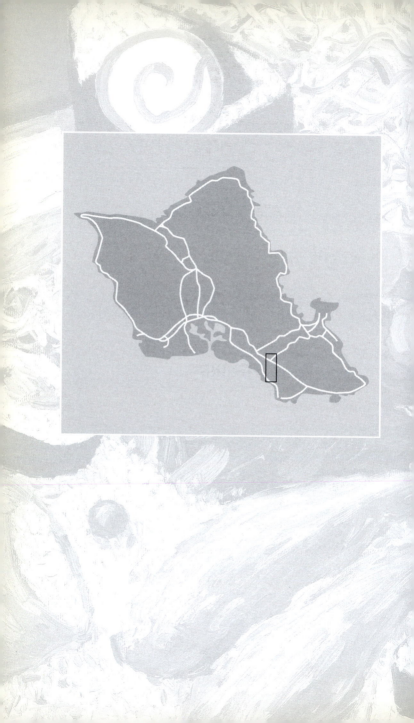

DOWNTOWN OKAZU

58 ALAKEA DELI

60 NEW WAVE KITCHEN

62 NUUANU OKAZU-YA

64 ROYDEN'S OKAZUYA
    & CATERING

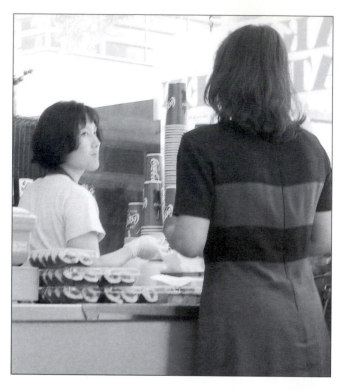

"When we took over the business, we tried to offer only Korean food, like kalbi, but found our customers wanted the okazu. We learned that offering both Korean food and okazu was the right combination that keeps our customers coming back."

Hyok Kwon

Alakea Deli

WHERE STAY?	201 South King Street Honolulu, Hawaii 96813 Phone 533-4666 (on the corner of King and Alakea streets in downtown Honolulu)
HOURS	Monday-Friday, 6 a.m. - 4 p.m. Saturday & Sunday, closed
GOTTA GRIND	Fried chicken, shoyu long rice, kinpira gobo, eggplant
BESIDES OKAZU	Korean plate lunch, Korean maki sushi
SEATING	Keep your eyes open! (one counter with barstools)
PARKING	Good luck! (no parking available, but if you work downtown, it's convenient)
CATERING?	Yes
ESTABLISHED	1997
NOTES	_____

"We work very hard to please our customers. Good food and good service is just the beginning."

Kiyoshi Nakasone

New Wave Kitchen

WHERE STAY?	568 Halekauwila Street Honolulu, Hawaii 96813 Phone 540-1010 (across First Circuit Court, next door to Royden's Okazuya)
HOURS	Monday-Friday, 9 a.m. - 2:30 p.m. Saturday & Sunday, closed
GOTTA GRIND	Garlic chicken, ahi poke, "Seafood Dynamite"
BESIDES OKAZU	Plate lunch, Hawaiian food, poke, kim chee
SEATING	Make house! (2 long tables — cafeteria style — and 1 small table)
PARKING	Happy hunting! (street parking only but a nice walk from downtown offices)
INSIDE SCOOPS	They close when food runs out — around 2 p.m. — so get there early for best selection.
CATERING?	Yes
ESTABLISHED	1998
NOTES	

"I love to cook and really enjoy eating. I love to share what we offer and see our customers' happy faces."

Yusei Nagamine

Nuuanu Okazu-Ya

WHERE STAY?
1351 Nuuanu Avenue
Honolulu, Hawaii 96817
Phone 533-6169
(between Vineyard Boulevard and
Kukui Street; across from Hosoi
Garden Mortuary)

HOURS
Tuesday-Saturday, 6 a.m. - 2 p.m.

GOTTA GRIND
Chow fun, fish cake items, kobu
maki, kinpira gobo

BESIDES OKAZU
Hamburger steak, pork tofu, saimin,
wonton min

SEATING
Keep your eyes open! (5 tables — but
they fill up fast)

PARKING
Happy hunting! (street parking only
but an easy stroll from downtown offices)

INSIDE SCOOPS
Closes for two weeks every year

CATERING?
No

ESTABLISHED
1978

NOTES
_____
_____
_____
_____
_____
_____
_____

*"Our storefront reads
'Royden's Okazuya and
Catering.' Some of our
customers — local
people — think
'Okazuya' is our last
name. It's hard to believe
they don't know what
'okazuya' means."*

Royden Oshita

Royden's Okazuya & Catering

WHERE STAY?
568 Halekauwila Street
Honolulu, Hawaii 96813
Phone 528-5029
(across First Circuit Court and
next door to New Wave Kitchen)

HOURS
Monday - Friday, opens 6 a.m.
Saturday & Sunday, closed

GOTTA GRIND
Sweet sour spareribs, shoyu butterfish,
Chinese fish cake, pork hash patties

BESIDES OKAZU
Chinese chicken salad, a variety of daily
plate lunch specials

SEATING
Make house! (3 tables and one long table)

PARKING
Happy hunting! (some street parking but
a nice walk from downtown offices)

INSIDE SCOOPS
They close when the food runs out —
about 1:30 p.m. — so get there early for
the best selection.

CATERING?
Yes

ESTABLISHED
1998

OKAZUYA TRIVIA
The owners are a brother-and-sister
team: Royden and Lori Oshita.

NOTES
_____

_____

_____

_____

_____

_____

_____

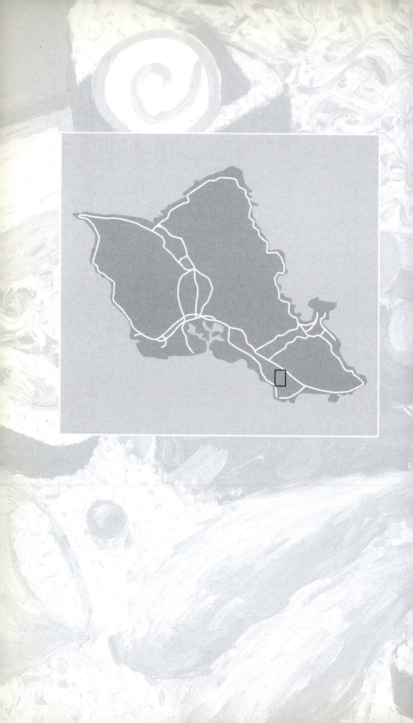

MIDTOWN OKAZU

68 CARYN'S OKAZUYA

70 EBISU CATERING SERVICE

72 ETHEL'S DELICATESSEN

74 GEORGE'S DELICATESSEN

76 MASA'S FOODS

78 SUEHIRO JAPANESE
RESTAURANT & CATERING

"I never saw myself doing this, but I love what I do and cooking food the way we like to eat it. Positive comments about what we offer really keep us going."

Sharlene Koga

Caryn's Okazuya

WHERE STAY? 1270 Young Street, # 1
Honolulu, Hawaii 96814
Phone 597-8083
(look for the green pompom on the pole
in front)

HOURS Monday, closed
Tuesday - Saturday, 6 a.m. - 2 p.m.
Sunday, closed

GOTTA GRIND Inari sushi, mochiko chicken, teri
mahi, eggplant/Spam tempura

SEATING Keep your eyes open! (4 tables — but
sometimes they fill up fast!)

PARKING No sweat! (large parking lot)

CATERING? Yes

ESTABLISHED 1940s (Sharlene Koga took over the
business in 1985. Caryn's has been in this
location since 1990.)

NOTES

"It feels like we bring back a sense of nostalgia. We still use brown paper wrap. We like to remember how it used to be."

Colleen Kuromoto

Ebisu Catering Service

WHERE STAY?	1915 South King Street Honolulu, Hawaii 96826 Phone 941-6055 (between Pumehana and McCully Streets, across Honolulu Craft Supply)
HOURS	Monday & Tuesday, 7 a.m. - 2:30 p.m. Wednesday, closed Thursday-Saturday, 7 a.m. - 2:30 p.m. Sunday, closed
GOTTA GRIND	Maki sushi, inari sushi, chow fun, teri chicken, nishime
BESIDES OKAZU	Okinawan sweet potato pie
SEATING	Take-out only! (We suggest you enjoy your okazu at nearby Old Stadium Park!)
PARKING	Good luck! (street parking in front of the shop)
INSIDE SCOOPS	Closes each year Jan. 1-7.
CATERING?	Yes
ESTABLISHED	1962
NOTES	

"Local people are the best because they love food!"

JoAnn Watts

Ethel's Delicatessen

WHERE STAY?	1495 South King Street Honolulu, Hawaii 96813 Phone 941-9057 (between Kaheka Street and Kalakaua Avenue; a few doors Diamond Head of the Kaheka Professional Center)
HOURS	Monday, closed Tuesday-Saturday, 4:30 a.m. - noon Sunday, closed
GOTTA GRIND	Fried chicken, inari sushi, maki sushi, hot dog sushi, stuffed tofu, stuffed eggplant, fishcake, kinpira gobo, chow fun
SEATING	Take-out only!
PARKING	No sweat! (3 metered stalls on King Street and parking in the back of the building — enter via Kaheka Street)
INSIDE SCOOPS	Closes for vacation the first week of January each year. They accept personal checks.
CATERING?	Yes (For small parties — to ensure that your order is filled, advance notice of one hour is required for most items.)
ESTABLISHED	1940s (current owner took over in 1975)
NOTES	

*"We really try to stick
to traditional home
cooking, like mama and
grandma used to make.
It's a lot of early hours
and hard work."*

Ron Ueda

George's Delicatessen

WHERE STAY?	1317 South Beretania Street Honolulu, Hawaii 96814 Phone 597-8069 (across Wong's Drapery)
HOURS	Monday-Saturday, 9 a.m. - 3 p.m. Sunday, closed
GOTTA GRIND	Maki sushi, inari sushi, mushroom chicken
BESIDES OKAZU	Plate lunch, saimin, Chinese dishes
SEATING	Keep your eyes open! (2 tables)
PARKING	Happy hunting! (street parking only — but there are usually open spaces nearby)
CATERING?	Yes
ESTABLISHED	1958 (at current location since 1977)
NOTES	

"I opened Masa's because I didn't like teaching — too much paperwork. So I have no menu or fax machine!"

Roland Okamura

Masa's Foods

WHERE STAY?	1325 South King Street Honolulu, Hawaii 96814 Phone 596-8166 (across Interstate Building next to the Trophy House)
HOURS	Monday-Friday, 6 a.m. - 1:45 p.m.
GOTTA GRIND	Korean chicken, baked ahi with crab, sweet sour spare ribs
BESIDES OKAZU	Plate lunch (including pot roast and mixed plate)
SEATING	Take-out only!
PARKING	Happy hunting! (street parking only)
INSIDE SCOOPS	The plate lunches are so popular, sometimes they run out of rice.
CATERING?	Yes
ESTABLISHED	1984
NOTES	

"The original owner was one of the first chefs from Japan invited to work in Hawaii. He wanted his own business so he started Suehiro Restaurant, which was smaller and a few blocks away. In 1975, he opened this restaurant. He retired but we still carry on his tradition."

Aki Saito

Suehiro Japanese Restaurant & Catering

WHERE STAY?   1824 South King Street
Honolulu, Hawaii 96826
Phone 949-4584
Fax 946-6529
(can't miss the large building with
the "Suehiro" fan logo, right before
Artesian Street)

HOURS   Daily, 9 a.m. - 8 p.m.
(Restaurant hours are Sunday-Thursday:
11 a.m. - 2 p.m. lunch; 5 - 9 p.m. dinner
and Friday & Saturday: 11 a.m. - 2 p.m.
lunch; 5-9:30 p.m. dinner)

GOTTA GRIND   Tempura, butterfish, short ribs

BESIDES OKAZU   Assortment of bento, shave ice,
donburi and udon. The okazuya window is
part of Suehiro Restaurant, which
features Japanese food. They also have
"Bentos to Go!" — free delivery with
50 or more bentos.

SEATING   Take-out only!

PARKING   No sweat! (large parking lot with
about 50 stalls)

INSIDE SCOOPS   It's cheaper to order the prepared bento
than to order a la carte. There are many
bento combinations to choose from.
VISA and MasterCard accepted.

CATERING?   Yes (for 10 or more people)

ESTABLISHED   1975

NOTES   _____

_____

_____

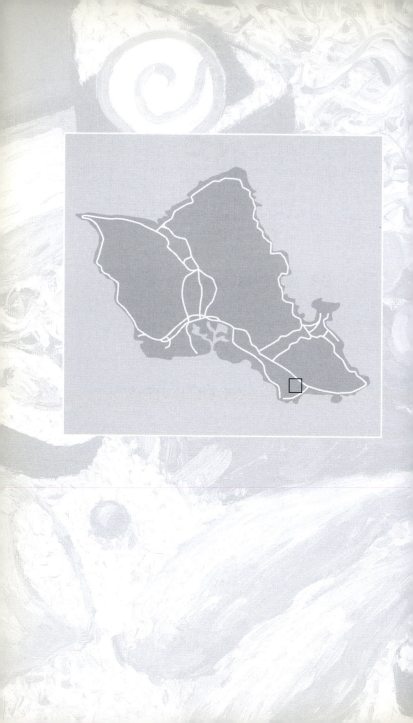

UPTOWN OKAZU

82 FUKUYA DELICATESSEN
      & CATERING

84 KAIMUKI SAIMIN & DELI

86 SEKIYA'S RESTAURANT
      & DELICATESSEN

88 ST. LOUIS DELICATESSEN

"My great-grandfather started this business, then my grandfather ran it, then my mom and dad, and now my wife and I are taking over."

Arrison Iwahiro

Fukuya Delicatessen & Catering

WHERE STAY?
2710 South King Street
Honolulu, Hawaii 96826
Phone 946-2073
(a few doors up King Street
from Puck's Alley)

HOURS
Monday & Tuesday, closed
Wednesday-Sunday, 6 a.m. - 2 p.m.

GOTTA GRIND
Sushi, chow fun, fried chicken, teri ahi,
mochiko chicken, miso butterfish, sea
burger, croquettes, BBQ/hotdog/chicken
rolls (great for a meal-on-the-go or a day
on the golf course), tofu dishes

BESIDES OKAZU
Mochi and cookies (order the cookies in
advance because they sell out fast)

SEATING
Keep your eyes open! (one table
and a long bench outside)

PARKING
Happy hunting! (6 stalls in front of the
building and street parking—metered
stalls, only during certain hours)

INSIDE SCOOPS
Closes for a two-week annual
vacation in early March. For purchases
more than $10, they accept VISA,
MasterCard and personal checks.

CATERING?
Yes

ESTABLISHED
1941 (opened by current owners' great-
grandparents; at this location since 1979)

NOTES

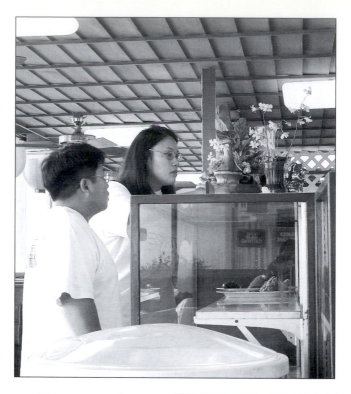

"My parents always wanted to start a family business. We're getting used to waking up early, really early."

Stanley Takara

Kaimuki Saimin & Deli

WHERE STAY? 3538 Waialae Avenue
Honolulu, Hawaii 96816
Phone 737-3939
(across Kaimuki District Park)

HOURS Daily, 6 a.m. - 2 p.m. (Dinner hours,
Friday & Saturday, 5:30 - 10 p.m.)

GOTTA GRIND Sushi, tofu patty, fish cake, fried chicken

BESIDES OKAZU Saimin, dine-in entrees

SEATING Make house! (13 tables)

PARKING Happy hunting! (6 stalls and
street parking)

INSIDE SCOOPS They sometimes run out of some items
around closing time, so get there early for
the best selection. Be sure to pick up a
frequent visitor card; after accumulating
$50 (a stamp for every $5) in purchases,
you'll receive $5 off the next purchase.

CATERING? Yes

ESTABLISHED 1997 (current owner took over in 2000)

NOTES _____

_____

_____

_____

_____

_____

_____

*"People often mistake the
hash balls for andagi.
But when they discover
what it really is,
they love it!*

Eddie Kaito

Sekiya's Restaurant & Delicatessen

WHERE STAY?
2746 Kaimuki Avenue
Honolulu, Hawaii 96816
Phone 732-1656
(across Kaimuki High School)

HOURS
Daily, 8:30 a.m. - 4:30 p.m.
Sekiya Restaurant hours:
Sunday, 8:30 a.m. - 10 p.m.
Monday-Thursday, 8:30 a.m. - 11 p.m.
Friday-Saturday, 8:30 a.m. - midnight

GOTTA GRIND
Fried saimin, shrimp tempura,
inari sushi, hash balls

BESIDES OKAZU
Oyako donburi, dine-in entrees

SEATING
Make house! Seating is available
inside the restaurant.

PARKING
No sweat! (large parking lot)

INSIDE SCOOPS
Closes for an annual vacation
in January. For those who love nostalgia,
Sekiya's is one of the few okazuyas that
can package your okazu in a paper bento
box. VISA and MasterCard accepted.

CATERING?
Yes (for small parties)

ESTABLISHED
1935 (at current location for more
than 40 years)

NOTES
_____

_____

_____

_____

_____

_____

A - 5.75	B - 5.00	MAKI SUSHI		CHOWFUN	.80
SUSHI	SUSHI	ROLL	3.00	LONG RICE	.80
MUSUBI	MUSUBI	PIECE	.50	NISHIME	.80
CHOWFUN	CHOWFUN	CONE SUSHI	.75	TOFU	.80
CHICKEN	CHICKEN			KOMBU	.80
LUNCHEON MEAT	LUNCHEON MEAT	MUSUBI		NAMASU	.50
POTATO	POTATO	PLAIN	.30	SALAD	.80
SHRIMP	SHRIMP	NORI	.40		
FISH					
		TEMPURA		LUNCHEON MEAT	
C - 4.00	MINI - 3.25	FISH	1.00	HOT DOG	
		SHRIMP	.60	HASH	
2 MUSUBI	MUSUBI	VEGETABLE	.60	TERIYAKI MEAT	
CHOWFUN	CHOWFUN	POTATO	.50	FRIED CHICKEN	
CHICKEN	CHICKEN			SHOYU CHICKEN	
LUNCHEON MEAT	LUNCHEON MEAT	SODA & JUICE	.00		
POTATO		BOTTLED WATER	.75		

"My husband's family had an okazuya in Kalihi, but it was too small. When the owner of St. Louis Delicatessen retired, my in-laws bought the business. This was a larger okazuya and a better location — plus we looked forward to all the school kids stopping by."

Lynn Higa

St. Louis Delicatessen

WHERE STAY?	3147 Waialae Avenue Honolulu, Hawaii 96816 Phone 732-0955 (across St. Louis School, next to St. Louis Drive-In)
HOURS	Monday, closed Tuesday-Saturday, 9 a.m. - 1:30 p.m. Sunday, closed
GOTTA GRIND	Chow fun, fried chicken, hash, inari sushi
BESIDES OKAZU	Assortment of bento
SEATING	Keep your eyes open! (a few outdoor tables)
PARKING	No sweat! (parking lot in front of the okazuya)
INSIDE SCOOPS	They close when the food runs out, so get there early for the best selection! The okazuya also closes every now and then when the owners "need a break."
CATERING?	No
ESTABLISHED	1950s (Tsutomu and Lynn Higa took over the business in 1993.)
NOTES	

WINDWARD OKAZU

92 BLOSSOM'S OKAZUYA

94 CHI-CHAN'S OKAZU-YA

96 GOHAN ETC.

98 KUULEI DELICATESSEN

100 MARUKI-TEI

102 MASA & JOYCE FISH MARKET

104 MASA & JOYCE II

"It's rough work and it can get very tiring, especially with the long and early hours, but we enjoy what we're doing."

Howard Ishikawa

Blossom's Okazuya

WHERE STAY?
1090 Keolu Drive, Suite 109
Kailua, Hawaii 96734
Phone 263-3338
Fax 263-5528
(in the same shopping center as Keolu
Center Cinemas - Wallace Theatres in
Enchanted Lake)

HOURS
Monday, closed
Tuesday-Friday, 6 a.m. - 6 p.m.
Saturday, 7 a.m. - 2 p.m.
Sunday, closed

GOTTA GRIND
Sesame chicken, maki sushi,
ginger-shoyu pork

BESIDES OKAZU
Bento, plate lunch, poke, fresh fish,
tako, sashimi

SEATING
Take-out only!

PARKING
No sweat! (shopping center parking lot)

INSIDE SCOOPS
They close when the food runs out, as
early as 1 p.m., so get there early for
the best selection!

CATERING?
Yes (for small parties)

ESTABLISHED
1990 (at current location since 1997)

NOTES
_____

_____

_____

_____

_____

_____

_____

"We live in town and didn't know much about Kaneohe till opening this business, and we've met so many nice people. My mom, Patricia Kochi, says she's made more friends than money and that's what's important. Even sumo wrestler Akebono ate here."

Chiemi Kochi

Chi-Chan's Okazu-ya

WHERE STAY?
45-1127 Kamehameha Highway
Kaneohe, Hawaii 96744
Phone 236-3000
(in the strip mall across American Savings
and Gohan Etc.)

HOURS
Monday, closed
Tuesday-Saturday, 6 a.m. - 12:30 p.m.
Sunday, closed

GOTTA GRIND
Chow fun, butterfish, kinpira gobo,
sesame chicken, konbu maki, Spam musubi

BESIDES OKAZU
Miso soup, saimin

SEATING
Keep your eyes open! (2 tables)

PARKING
No sweat! (large parking lot)

INSIDE SCOOPS
They close when the food runs out, so
get there early for the best selection!
The chow fun is so popular, it usually runs
out by 7 a.m. They don't accept bills $50
or larger. Closes for two weeks during
the spring and fall.

CATERING?
Yes

ESTABLISHED
1991

NOTES
_____

_____

_____

_____

_____

_____

_____

"My husband, Brian, was a teppanyaki chef and went to cooking school on the mainland. We always wanted to open a restaurant and saw this okazuya as a good stepping stone. He can cook all kinds of food, and for now this is perfect."

Darryln Nakamura

Gohan Etc.

WHERE STAY?	45-1048 Kamehameha Highway, Suite C Kaneohe, Hawaii 96744 Phone 247-7423 (same building as Kaneohe Farm Supply; across Chi-Chan's Okazu-ya)
HOURS	Monday, closed Tuesday-Saturday, 6 a.m. - 2 p.m. Sunday, closed
GOTTA GRIND	Garlic chicken, nori chicken, corned beef hash
BESIDES OKAZU	Filipino dishes (pork adobo, lechon kawali — orders come from as far away as Ewa Beach!), plate lunch (roast turkey)
SEATING	Keep your eyes open! (2 tables)
PARKING	No sweat! (large parking lot)
INSIDE SCOOPS	Closes for annual vacation sometime in August
CATERING?	Yes
ESTABLISHED	1998
NOTES	

"My husband and I are originally from Japan. And you won't find 'okazuyas' in Japan. The okazuya is local — the food is different from Japanese food. My customers taught me how to cook this way — if I make and they don't like it, I try again until they like it."

Miyoko Kochi

Kuulei Delicatessen

WHERE STAY?
418 Kuulei Road
Kailua, Hawaii 96734
Phone 261-5321
(next to the Shell gas station at the
entrance of Kailua town on the corner of
Oneawa Street and Kuulei Road)

HOURS
Monday, 6:30 a.m. - 1 p.m.
Tuesday, closed
Wednesday-Sunday, 6:30 a.m. - 1 p.m.

GOTTA GRIND
Long rice, fried chicken, shrimp and sweet
potato tempura

SEATING
Make house! (6 tables)

PARKING
Good luck! (street parking only)

INSIDE SCOOPS
Closes for one week after New Year's.
Personal checks accepted.

CATERING?
No

ESTABLISHED
1972

NOTES

_____

_____

_____

_____

_____

_____

_____

*"The logo's kanji
character means
'happiness' and the circle
around it signifies
'complete.' We hope our
customers are completely
happy when they
enjoy our okazu."*

Eloise Holt

Maruki-Tei

WHERE STAY?   Windward Mall
46-056 Kamehameha Highway
Kaneohe, Hawaii 96744
Phone 235-4445

HOURS   Monday-Saturday, 10 a.m. - 9 p.m.
(okazu section closes at 8 p.m.)
Sunday, 10 a.m. - 5 p.m.

GOTTA GRIND   Sesame chicken, sushi, tempura,
mac/potato salad

BESIDES OKAZU   Plate lunch (beef stew, saimin, sweet sour
spare ribs, chicken tofu with long rice,
etc.), Hawaiian food

SEATING   Make house! (6 tables and seats on the
counter — and of course, places to sit
in the mall)

PARKING   No sweat! (Windward Mall parking lot)

INSIDE SCOOPS   They continue to replenish the food
throughout the day.

CATERING?   Yes

ESTABLISHED   1982

OKAZUYA TRIVIA   The saimin soup is made with their
"old-fashioned" recipe.

NOTES   _____

_____

_____

_____

_____

_____

_____

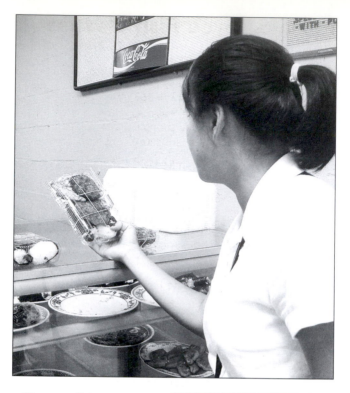

"I was a fisherman and my wife loves to cook, so we combined our talents and opened our shop."

Masa Tobaru

Masa & Joyce Fish Market

WHERE STAY?
Koolau Center
47-388 Hui Iwa Street
Kaneohe, Hawaii 96744
Phone 239-6966
(in the same shopping complex as the
Koolau Consolidated Theatres)

HOURS
Monday - Thursday, 8 a.m. - 6 p.m.
Friday & Saturday, 8 a.m. - 7 p.m.
Sunday, 8 a.m. - 5 p.m.

GOTTA GRIND
Chicken katsu, ahi patty, California roll,
lup cheong musubi, fried rice musubi,
hot dog/Spam musubi (the musubis are
huge!), teri chicken bits, hash

BESIDES OKAZU
Hawaiian plate lunch, beef stew,
tripe stew, sashimi, poke

SEATING
Keep your eyes open! (one table)

PARKING
No sweat! (large parking lot)

INSIDE SCOOPS
Closed the first week in January.
VISA, MasterCard and personal
checks accepted.

CATERING?
Yes

ESTABLISHED
1978

NOTES
_____
_____
_____
_____
_____
_____
_____

"I grew up working in the business, and it's become a way of life I truly enjoy."

Cynthia Tobaru

Masa & Joyce II

WHERE STAY?	45-582 Kamehameha Highway Kaneohe, Hawaii 96744 Phone 235-6129 (by Koolau Farmers and Kin Wah Chinese restaurant)
HOURS	Monday, Wednesday - Friday, 9 a.m. - 6 p.m. Tuesday, closed Saturday, 9 a.m. - 4 p.m. Sunday, 9 a.m. - 8 p.m.
GOTTA GRIND	Ahi patty, California roll, fried rice musubi, hot dog/Spam musubi (the musubis are huge!), teri chicken bits, hash
BESIDES OKAZU	Hawaiian plate lunch, sashimi, poke, andagi
SEATING	Make house! (6 tables)
PARKING	No sweat! (large parking lot)
INSIDE SCOOPS	Closed the first week in January. VISA, MasterCard and personal checks accepted.
CATERING?	Yes
ESTABLISHED	1984
NOTES	

INDEX

Alakea Deli	58
Blossom's Okazuya	92
Caryn's Okazuya	68
Chi-Chan's Okazu-ya	94
Ebisu Catering Service	70
Ethel's Delicatessen	72
Fukuya Delicatessen & Catering	82
George's Delicatessen	74
Gohan Etc.	96
Gulick Delicatessen & Coffee Shop	38
Kabuki Restaurant & Delicatessen	24
Kaimuki Saimin & Deli	84
Kawakami Delicatessen	40
Kitchen Delight	14
Kuulei Delicatessen	98
Maru-Hi Restaurant & Lounge	16
Maruki-Tei	100
Masa & Joyce Fish Market	102
Masa & Joyce II	104
Masa's Foods	76
Masago's Drive Inn	26
Mitsu-Ken Okazu & Catering	42
Mitsuba Delicatessen	44
Naru's Place	18
New Wave Kitchen	60
Nicky BBQ & Okazu	46
North Shore Country Okazu & Bento	10
Nuuanu Okazu-Ya	62
Okawa's Okazuya	48
Omiya's Restaurant	28
Royden's Okazuya & Catering	64
Sagara Store	12
Sakura Japanese Delicatessen & Catering	30
Sato's Okazuya	32
Sekiya's Restaurant & Delicatessen	86
St. Louis Delicatessen	88
Suehiro Japanese Restaurant & Catering	78
Sugoi	50
Sun's Bar-B-Q	20
Toshi's Delicatessen & Restaurant	52
Waipahu Deli	34
Yuki's Coffee House	54